RODB

G000252306

VET
ADVICE ON

LAMINITIS

IN HORSES

Rebecca Hamilton-Fletcher
BVSc (Hons), MRCVS

RODBASTON COLLEGE

00013400

ABOUT THE AUTHOR

Rebecca Hamilton-Fletcher qualified from Bristol University Veterinary School with Honours in 1983 and has since specialised in equine veterinary work. During this time, she has worked exclusively with racehorses and has also run her own ambulatory equine practice. She is now part of a large equine referral hospital in Salisbury, Wiltshire.

Rebecca is married to another equine vet and has one daughter. She produces and shows hunters at county level, and also does the 'pony club rounds' with her daughter, Bethany. She is a qualified riding instructor, and has been a regular veterinary correspondent for *Horse and Hound* magazine since 1996.

Some 35 years ago, Rebecca's first pony, Twinkle, became afflicted with chronic laminitis and battled heroically with it for many years. Relatively little was understood about the condition at that time, and attempts at treatment were frequently hopeless. Although Rebecca's work now involves all aspects of performance horse-related problems, Twinkle will never be forgotten, and laminitis remains a condition close to Rebecca's heart.

ACKNOWLEDGEMENTS

Viv Rainsbury: illustrations (pages 5, 9, 28, 34, 38). Rebecca Hamilton Fletcher: photography (pages 3, 19, 22, 23, 28, 29, 38).

**Published by Ringpress Books,
a division of Interpet Publishing,
Vincent Lane, Dorking, Surrey, RH4 3YX, UK.
Tel: 01306 873822   Fax: 01306 876712
email: sales@interpet.co.uk**

First published 2004
© 2004 Ringpress Books. All rights reserved.

No part of this book may be reproduced or transmitted in any form or by any means, electronic or mechanical, including photocopying, recording, or by any information storage and retrieval system, without permission in writing from the publisher.

ISBN 1 86054 247 6

Printed and bound in Singapore by Kyodo Printing

10 9 8 7 6 5 4 3 2 1

CONTENTS

Introduction

Laminitis is basically a failure of the attachment between the pedal bone in the foot (also known as the distal phalanx or coffin bone) and the inner hoof wall (see illustration opposite). This results in unrelenting pain, a characteristic lameness, and potentially irreversible damage to the horse's foot.

Laminitis has been recognised as a major medical concern within the horse industry for many centuries. As far back as 350BC it was described as Barley Disease by the early Greeks. Most people still associate laminitis with fat, native ponies stuffing themselves on rich pasture. The reality is that laminitis can affect any type of horse, pony or donkey, and at any time. The condition is extremely complex, with many, apparently unrelated, predisposing factors and causes.

Laminitis itself is rarely fatal. The fear that elevates the importance of this condition above other, more often life-threatening illnesses, such as colic, is based on the potential it has to deform horses' feet and cripple them for the rest of their painful lives – without actually killing them.

This book sets out to try to help you understand laminitis – what it is and why it occurs. It aims to teach the horse owner how to recognise the tell-tale signs and so seek veterinary advice as soon as possible, thereby improving the animal's chances of recovery. Even more importantly, it aims to put the owner in a position where he or she can take steps to prevent laminitis from developing in the first place.

1 What is laminitis?

To understand how laminitis affects the horse, it is necessary to understand how the normal, healthy foot is built and how it functions.

The pedal bone is equivalent to the last digit of the middle finger or toe on each of our limbs. It is covered in sensitive dermal laminae (like the quick of our nails) and lies suspended within the hoof wall capsule (equivalent to our nail), by means of interlocking with the hoof's lining of insensitive epidermal laminae.

All of these structures are nourished by a complex system of arteries, capillaries and veins that branch throughout the sensitive laminae around the pedal

CROSS-SECTION OF A NORMAL FOOT

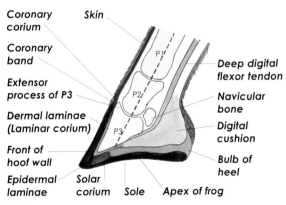

Coronary corium
Skin
Coronary band
Extensor process of P3
Dermal laminae (Laminar corium)
Front of hoof wall
Epidermal laminae
Solar corium
Sole
Apex of frog

P1
P2
P3

Deep digital flexor tendon
Navicular bone
Digital cushion
Bulb of heel

NOTES:
- P1, P2 and P3 are the three phalanges, with P3 being the pedal bone.
- P1, P2 and P3 should lie in a straight line.
- The front surface of P3 should be parallel to the front of the hoof wall.
- The top of the extensor process of P3 should lie slightly below the top of the hoof wall.
- The sole should be concave.

bone, as well as between the pedal bone and the sole.

New horn is produced by the coronary corium at the top of the hoof, and grows down slowly over a period of months. The deep digital flexor tendon runs down the back of the leg, where it attaches to the back of the pedal bone. The weight of the horse is transferred down the limb to the pedal bone. Here, it is transmitted by the interlocking laminae to the hoof wall, and then the ground. This is carried out with maximum efficiency if the anatomy of the lower limb conforms with certain 'ideal guidelines' (see notes to illustration on page 5).

THE PROCESS OF LAMINITIS

Laminitis is essentially the inflammation and subsequent tearing of the interlaminar locking system that suspends the pedal bone within the hoof capsule. It is caused by a disruption of the normal blood flow within the foot, and is extremely painful. In severe cases the suspension begins to break down, allowing the pedal bone to rotate or even sink. Various stages, or phases, in the disease process are recognised: developmental, acute, and chronic (or founder).

DEVELOPMENTAL PHASE

In this stage, changes begin to appear in the foot – but it can be hours, or even days, before the signs characteristic of laminitis develop. This is unfortunate, as it is only during the developmental phase that prevention is truly possible.

There are two general pathways by which laminitis has been proposed to occur:

Toxic, metabolic or enzymatic theory

Following a problem, such as an injury or illness, to some other part of the body (discussed later), a 'trigger factor', which is as yet unidentified, is released into the blood system and circulates around the body. It is thought to activate an enzyme ('MMP') that initiates the disruption of the interlaminar locking system. Many of the vascular changes described in the second hypothesis are then thought to follow.

Vascular theory
This theory proposes that the primary problem is a reduction in the blood flow to the feet (early digital hypo-perfusion). The capillaries in the laminae constrict, forcing fluid out into the spaces within the laminae, increasing pressure within the hoof capsule, until, eventually, the capillary blood-flow system becomes compromised. The formation of blood clots in the damaged capillaries further increases the chances of them becoming permanently blocked. 'Shunts' are formed to bypass this area of resistance, and, as a result of being starved of oxygen and nutrition, the laminae become ischaemic (i.e. die) and separate.

ACUTE PHASE
This is the stage when the level of inflammation and ischaemia is sufficient to cause pain and lameness. The acute phase is usually relatively short (20-72 hours), and will follow one of two courses:
- If the damage is very mild, a rapid and complete recovery is still possible with no lasting effects to the foot. In other cases, some six to nine months may be needed for the damage to repair fully, and, during this time, the horse is at an increased risk of developing acute laminitis again.
- If the level of ischaemia has been extensive and prolonged, sufficient damage will have occurred to the attachments between the pedal bone and the

hoof wall capsule for them to tear apart. The pedal bone will then begin to become displaced, by rotating with its toe downwards (known as 'founder').

If horses with acute laminitis are recognised, and treated immediately and appropriately, up to 85 per cent will make a full recovery, with as few as 15 per cent becoming chronic, long-term cases.

CHRONIC PHASE (FOUNDER)

A horse is said to have foundered if the interlaminar locking system has broken down sufficiently to allow the pedal bone to become displaced within the hoof.

There are five interrelated consequences of founder to consider. They tend to lead on from each other, and, together, they contribute to the chronic nature of the condition.

Mechanical failure

The breakdown in the pedal bone/hoof capsule relationship is probably the most important factor. As the pedal bone begins to rotate, the weakened interlaminar bonds are under pressure to stretch and tear still further. This weakening is aggravated by:

- The weight of the horse descending through P3.
- The increasing levels of ischaemia.
- The leakage of fluid from the damaged blood vessels creating still more pressure.
- The contraction of the deep digital flexor tendon and subsequent pulling upwards of the heel of P3.

As the link between P3 and the hoof wall is lost, the horse's weight is borne more by the pedal bone and the sole, rather than by the hoof wall. P3 and the sole are not designed to weight-bear, and they inevitably collapse under these demands.

CROSS SECTION OF AN ACUTELY FOUNDERED FOOT

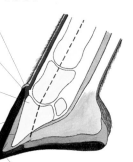

Coronary depression palpable here

Displaced and compressed coronary corium

Extensor process now significantly lower than coronary band

Fronts of P3 and hoof wall no longer parallel

Area of stretching and tearing of laminae now filling with serum and blood

Pressure of tip of P3 causing compression of solar blood vessels and flattening of sole (painful on palpation)

NOTES:
* The line through P1, P2 and P3 is no longer straight.
* The front of P3 is no longer parallel to the front of the hoof wall.
* The extensor process is now lower than it should be, relative to the coronary band, creating a depression at the front.
* The coronary corium at the top has been displaced so that new horn growth emerges at the wrong angle, creating a deformed appearance.
* The sole begins to drop due to the pressure of P3 above.
* The deep digital flexor tendon begins to contract to accommodate its new shorter length.
* As the situation worsens, P3 keeps rotating and the sole continues to flatten until eventually it becomes convex.
* Ultimately, P3 can penetrate through the sole, usually just in front of the point of the frog; this is known as a solar prolapse and is very serious.

Circulatory failure

As the foot collapses, the vascular supply is further torn and disrupted, with various outcomes:

* The laminar tissues become 'starved', leading to further ischaemic necrosis.
* Additional haemorrhage causes a further increase in pressure, and, therefore, pain, in the foot.
* Compression of the blood vessels between the sole and the bottom of P3 leads to bedsore-type lesions.

These can be seen as crescent-shaped bruises on the sole between the point of the frog and the toe.

- Sometimes, the sensitive blood vessels at the top of the hoof leak into the horn. If the foot is white, a bruise can be seen as a red ring growing down the foot over the next few months.
- Where there has been tearing of the laminae, a partial separation (seen as a honeycomb appearance around the perimeter of the sole) may remain always.
- There appears to be an element of circulatory hypersensitivity such that future episodes of acute laminitis are more likely. With each subsequent attack, additional damage is done and the animal becomes even more susceptible to circulatory problems in the foot.

Growth problems

- Laminitis stimulates an increased rate of horn growth.
- The coronary corium has become compressed at the front of the hoof, and the rate of growth is slower here compared to that of the heels.
- Due to the faster growth of the heels, over time, the foot assumes a slipper shape.

Various consequences follow on from this:

- The rings visible on the hoof wall will be different from normal growth rings, as they will be closer at the front and will diverge at the heels (normal growth rings should be the same distance apart all the way round the foot).
- There is a reduction in the total surface area of laminar interface, leading to further pedal bone/hoof wall instability.
- The horn quality is poor, adding to the general weakness of the foot.

- As the foot becomes ever more deformed, it becomes even more difficult (and painful) for the horse to walk normally. The horse will try to compensate for this by bearing weight on other areas, and this, in turn, will lead to further problems.

Infection

Wherever fluid has leaked out of the circulation, or where there has been bruising or laminar separation, there is an increased risk of infection. The risk is especially high if there has been a solar prolapse, but fortunately, these are rare. More common are cases of infecction tracking up the white line area (known as 'seedy toe'), or spreading throughout the solar corium (known as underrrunning of the sole – see diagram on page 5), or of more localised foot abscesses.

Pain

There are long-term implications for pain:
- The deep digital flexor tendon becomes shortened and contracted, so preventing the pedal bone from returning to its correct position.
- The hoof itself starts to contract, especially at the heels, causing additional inflammation and pain.
- As with any chronic lameness, secondary musculo-skeletal problems arise elsewhere in the body, due to the horse trying to hold and carry itself in an abnormal manner – back problems are common.

SINKERS

If a founder is so extensive that all the laminae have become detached, the pedal bone is effectively loose within the hoof. It drops to rest entirely on the sole, cutting off the blood supply there (known as a 'sinker' and potentially one of the most serious complications).

2 Causes of laminitis

Of the many myths surrounding laminitis, one of the most common assumptions is that the disease affects only those animals that live off rich pasture. This is a dangerous simplification. While horses on rich pasture may be more prone, laminitis can strike any horse (including ponies and donkeys), regardless of its exact age, its breed or the season. Although, the exact causes of laminitis remain poorly understood, there are a number of conditions involving other parts of the horse's body that predispose it towards developing the illness:

- Breed and obesity
- Age
- Diet
- Concussion
- Excess or prolonged weight-bearing on one leg
- Severe infection or illness
- Toxaemia or poisoning
- Sudden crisis/stress
- Metabolic disorders
- Drug-induced
- Environmental factors
- Immune hypersensitivity
- Miscellaneous/unknown.

BREED AND OBESITY

There is no real breed or sex predisposition for laminitis, but fat or obese animals are especially at risk. There is a metabolic difference between ponies and horses, in that ponies and cobs utilise their food more efficiently and so tend to put weight on more easily, making them more at risk of developing a dietary-based laminitis.

Owners are constantly under pressure to overfeed their animals due to:

- The fashion of having show animals fat, instead of fit.
- Advice from feed companies keen to sell products.
- Peer pressure.
- Modern pasture management leading to over-rich grazing for animals designed to survive on much less.

The result is that, in most cases, it is not the breed or type of animal that is ultimately responsible, but the management. However, a recently recognised syndrome, called 'obesity and laminitis syndrome', has now been noted, in which occasionally the management does *not* appear to be the main culprit.

AGE

Laminitis occurs mostly in mature horses. It is rarely found in animals less than a year old.

DIET

Horses are designed to eat little and often, for 18-20 hours a day. Their digestive system is designed to deal with a diet based on fibre. In the modern world, horses are more often maintained on concentrated foods and greatly reduced amounts of roughage, or on pastures that are rich and lush.

Laminitis can arise as a result of:

- The wrong type of food being fed (e.g. a native pony feeding on modern pasture).
- A sudden, massive intake of a 'high-risk' food (e.g. a horse breaking into the feed bins – known as 'grain overload').

PROTEINS AND CARBOHYDRATES

In the past, it was considered that it was protein levels in a food that determined whether or not it was 'high risk'. Now we know that proteins have little to do with laminitis, and that it is the total weight of soluble carbohydrates consumed that is the critical factor.

Carbohydrates consist of sugars (simple carbohydrates, such as glucose, fructose and lactose) and non-sugars (complex, soluble, energy-storage carbohydrates, such as starch present in cereals and fructans present in plants).

It is the non-sugars that can lead to laminitis. They are poorly digested in the stomach and small intestines, and, if an excessively large amount has been consumed, they will spill over undigested into the hind-gut. Here, they bring about a chain of events:

- 'Undesirable' or 'bad' gut bacteria, which relish this type of carbohydrate, multiply rapidly, at the expense of 'desirable' or 'good' bacteria.
- These bad bacteria produce an excess of lactic acid and volatile fatty acids, creating an acid environment in the gut, which can damage the gut lining.
- The good bacteria, killed off by the overgrowth of bad bacteria and by the sudden acidity in the gut, release poisons called endotoxins as they die.
- These endotoxins can pass through the damaged gut wall into the blood stream, making the animal ill (although this does not cause laminitis itself).
- Bad bacteria also produce a poison called an exotoxin.
- Exotoxin is also able to pass into the blood stream via the damaged lining of the gut.
- It is thought that these exotoxins could be the trigger factor that stimulates the destructive MMP enzymes in the foot, causing laminitis.

It can be seen, therefore, that the level of soluble carbohydrates in the diet should be carefully monitored. This is relatively easy when dealing with cereal-based compound feeds, as they contain known amounts of starch. It is more difficult to assess how high the fructan concentration is in the grass at any one time.

Fructans

Fructans are produced as a result of photosynthesis. This process, which requires the presence of carbon dioxide, water and sunlight, is necessary for growth. Sucrose (simple sugar) is produced first, and it represents the plant's immediate source of energy. If conditions are favourable, photosynthesis continues and fructans are produced. These are stored within the plant to be used as a source of energy should the supply of sucrose become depleted.

There are many factors influencing the concentration of fructans in the plant, including the type of grass, part of plant, age of plant, temperature, season, light intensity, and the presence of water or other plants or herbicides. This large number of factors means that fructan concentration can vary enormously – even from hour to hour – and this can make it very difficult to predict the times of greatest risk. However, some generalisations can be made:

- If the weather is cool and sunny, the fructan concentration tends to be higher.
- If the weather is dull and overcast, the concentration tends to be lower.
- Cold, frosty, sunny mornings tend to be among the highest risk times.
- Stems tend to have the highest fructan concentration of a plant, hence grazing on stubble can represent a greater risk than grazing on longer, leafier grass.

- Grass is especially high in fructans in the spring and autumn, when most growing occurs.

By appreciating the role that soluble carbohydrates have to play, owners can help to reduce the risks involved in grazing susceptible animals, especially in the spring and autumn, without having to resort to the rather drastic method of keeping them off grass altogether (see Chapter Five).

CONCUSSION

Concussion, also known as 'road founder' and 'concussion laminitis', is a commonly recognised form of traumatic or mechanical laminitis, but is probably also the least understood. It is thought that excessive concussion can cause traumatic tearing of the laminae, leading to constriction of the capillaries, reduced perfusion, inflammation within the foot, and, ultimately, structural collapse.

Typical situations leading to concussion laminitis include:
- Driving ponies, hammering on the hard ground.
- Jumping/galloping on hard ground in the summer.
- Summer racehorses.
- Inadequately fit endurance horses.
- Heavy horses working on hard surfaces – it is established that horses over 87 stones/1212 lbs (550 kgs) are twice as susceptible to this form of laminitis.

The shape of the foot, the conformation of the lower limb and the quality of the hoof wall, can also be factors. Animals with long toes and low heels (e.g. Thoroughbreds) are more susceptible. Good foot care is essential – a degree of concussion laminitis is seen sometimes after severe trimming or improper shoeing.

EXCESSIVE OR PROLONGED WEIGHT-BEARING ON ONE LEG

In reality, this is another form of concussion laminitis. It can occur if the animal is suffering from a severe long-term lameness in one leg, so that the other front or back leg has to support significantly more than its fair share of weight. It can also be a complication of surgery that has resulted in one leg being in a cast and therefore unable to weight-bear.

It is estimated that the risks increase significantly for any lameness lasting longer than three weeks, and the heavier the animal, the more susceptible it is.

SEVERE INFECTION OR ILLNESS

Any systemic disease can result in laminitis, but some conditions are known to be particularly high risk:

- Retained placenta leading to endometritis
- Pneumonia
- Colitis
- Pleuritis
- Diarrhoea.

TOXAEMIA OR POISONING

These can cause vascular damage and blood-clotting disturbances, leading potentially to decreased blood flow to the feet. Toxins can be:

- Viral
- Bacterial
- Fungal
- Chemical
- Plant-derived.

SUDDEN CRISIS/STRESS

Stress stimulates the adrenal glands, creating increased levels of circulating corticosteroids. Once in the foot, these can have destructive effects on the circulation.

Examples of such situations include:

- Severe colic
- Massive haemorrhage
- Shock
- Complications following surgery
- Prolonged journeys, especially in extreme weather.

METABOLIC DISORDERS

Any form of kidney or liver dysfunction can affect metabolism and ultimately contribute to laminitis. One of the most frequently recognised conditions that has laminitis as a consequence is Cushing's disease.

CUSHING'S DISEASE

Cushing's disease occurs when a benign growth forms on the pituitary gland at the base of the brain, usually in the older animal. It results in an excess of the glucocorticoid steroid in the blood, leading to a variety of secondary problems:

- Loss of condition and muscle wastage
- Excessive drinking
- Long, matted, shaggy coat all year round
- Persistent sweating for no apparent reason
- Lethargy
- Bulging eyes
- An increased susceptibility to secondary infections
- Laminitis.

Diagnosis of Cushing's disease can be confirmed with blood tests. Fortunately, medical treatment for this condition is possible. However, it is expensive and it will not cure the problem. Ultimately, the condition will progress until the decision is made for euthanasia on humane grounds.

This Shetland Pony has Cushing's disease. Note the shaggy, curly coat, marked sweating and the laminitic feet.

HYPOTHYROIDISM

It has often been proposed that a degree of hypothyroidism can be involved in laminitis, although it has never been proved. Supplementation with thyroid precursors is still practised in some cases, and does seem to be of benefit occasionally.

INSULIN INSENSITIVITY IN PONIES

There is an undeniable link between insulin, obesity and laminitis. Insulin is produced by the body in response to glucose entering the blood after eating. In some obese ponies even more insulin is required, due to an acquired insensitivity. Excessively high levels of insulin can have a direct effect on the blood supply to the foot, which, in combination with the stresses created by the animal's obesity, can result in laminitis.

DRUG-INDUCED

Certain drugs carry a risk of triggering laminitis in already susceptible animals. Corticosteroids, classically given to fat, grass-fed ponies in the summer to provide them some relief from sweet itch, can cause a quick and serious episode of acute laminitis, which may progress to sinking (see page 11) within hours. Vets are now reluctant to use certain forms of steroids in high-risk animals, unless it is essential.

ENVIRONMENTAL FACTORS

The levels of fructans in grass can be greatly influenced by the weather – with cold nights and sunny days creating especially high-risk conditions (see page 15).

IMMUNE HYPERSENSITIVITY

Studies have shown that some animals that founder also develop an increased sensitivity to their own immune system. This causes them to produce an abnormally intense and prolonged allergic-type response to certain allergens (substances, usually naturally occuring in the environment, which can trigger allergic-type reactions in particular individuals). This was thought to explain the reports of episodes of acute laminitis in otherwise apparently healthy animals following routine procedures (such as worming and vaccination), or the application of certain sarcoid creams. However, this has turned out not to be clear-cut. On investigation, many of these animals already had a level of pre-existing chronic laminitis.

However, the fact remains that foundered animals can sometimes react bizarrely to certain stimuli – with cases of apparently spontaneous urticaria (skin rash) often being recognised.

MISCELLANEOUS/UNKNOWN

As with any complex disease, there are always going to be those cases for which no reason or cause can be found. They remain supremely frustrating to deal with.

3 Diagnosis of laminitis

L aminitis produces a range of symptoms. Sometimes the picture can be further complicated by the coexistence of another primary condition or illness, such as Cushing's disease.

It is important to remember that laminitis can affect just one limb, or all four of them. The front feet are most commonly affected. Laminitis can appear very quickly, with severe symptoms (acute laminitis – see Chapter One), or it can appear more gradually, over a period of time, in which case it is often a relapse from a previous acute episode.

SYMPTOMS OF ACUTE LAMINITIS

Pain in the feet, manifested as lameness, is the primary symptom. It can vary hugely, from very mild to severe. However, in all cases, the lameness is more apparent on a hard surface and on the turn. Characteristics depend on the degree of severity and may include:

- Apparent normality at walk, but short and stilted at the trot, with a 'heel before toe' gait; or a short, stilted walk and a reluctance to trot.
- A preference to pivot on the hind quarters rather than to walk forwards.
- An obvious reluctance to move, with resistance to have a foot lifted.
- 'Sinkers' refuse to move at all, and may choose to spend much of their time lying down. If forced to walk, they move in a flat-footed manner, 'slapping' their feet down characteristically (the pedal bone being effectively 'loose' inside the hoof).

Welsh Pony showing some typical characteristics of laminitis affecting all four feet – trying to take weight off the front feet, shifting from one foot to the other, rocking back on the heels, and an 'anxious' expression.

When the horse is stationary, it will adopt a characteristic laminitic stance, which can be likened to having all four feet 'nailed to the floor':

- Rocks back on heels, to take weight off toes.
- Stretches forelegs out in front.
- Tries to support most of its weight on its hind legs by tucking its hind quarters underneath it.
- On the rare occasion of a hind-limb laminitis, the horse will stand with the hind legs stretched out behind it, as if trying to urinate. Owners will often mistake this for signs of kidney disease.
- Repeatedly shifts its weight from foot to foot, and incessantly lifts one leg up, then the other.
- Assumes an 'anxious' expression.
- The most severe cases lie down, groaning and sweating. They may become cast. Many owners believe them to have colic or a broken back, or to have 'tied up'.
- There will be a bounding digital pulse. This can be

felt by palpating the digital artery as it passes over the back and sides of the fetlock joint. Get used to the feel of the pulse in the normal horse, but remember that an increased digital pulse could be due to an infection (e.g. pus in the foot) or some other cause of inflammation, and not just laminitis.

- There may be a depression at the coronary band. Again, get used to the normal feel of this area by running your finger down the front of the pastern, over the coronary band, and on to the hoof wall. If a dip is present, just above the coronet, it suggests a degree of founder; the deeper and more extensive and painful the depression round the sides of the foot, the worse the founder. If the depression runs all the way round, the horse is probably a sinker.
- The horse will resent pressure to the sole, between the toe of the foot and the point of the frog.
- A large neck crest will feel firmer and tauter in laminitic ponies.
- Heat in the foot is not a consistent finding and should not be relied on.

 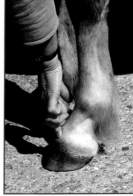

Where to check for the digital pulse (left) and the coronary band depression (right).

ADDITIONAL SYMPTOMS OF CHRONIC LAMINITIS

- 'Aladdin's slipper' foot shape, with a long toe and a concave front wall.
- Divergent growth rings, which are wider at the heels (where the rate of new horn growth is quicker) and closer at the front of the foot.
- Tendency towards a flat or convex sole.
- Widening of the white line, giving a honeycomb appearance when viewed from below, especially in the toe region.
- Tendency to suffer from bruised soles, solar abscesses or 'seedy toe' (infection within the white line).
- Signs of Cushing's disease in the older animal.

WHAT SHOULD YOU DO?

Laminitis is a medical emergency; if your horse or pony is showing any of the above symptoms, call your vet immediately. The chances of a full recovery are greatly improved if treatment is started early.

While you are waiting for the vet to arrive:

- Remove your horse from the cause, if known (e.g. lush grass) and stable him.
- Avoid walking any distance – if the stable is some way away, use a low-loading trailer instead.
- If the horse refuses to move, stay with it until the vet arrives – do not allow grazing.
- Commence complete box rest. Ideally, the stable should be quite large. Having to turn tightly is very painful for laminitic animals. Stable the horse on a deep, clean bed of shavings, paper or sand. Deep littering is not a good idea as the chemical build-up in a wet base is damaging to the horn of the hoof (as well as to the lungs).
- Encourage the horse to lie down as much as possible to take the weight off the feet.

- Keep the immediate environment as stress-free as possible by having it quiet and dark, and by using aids such as air conditioners, heaters and dehumidifiers – these will all help the horse to relax and to rest.
- Remove all food in the short term (but make sure there is fresh water available). However, do not be tempted to starve your horse in the longer term, as this could induce a serious, potentially fatal, condition called hyperlipaemia. This occurs when fat is mobilised from stores in the body to provide energy, in response to a sudden lack of food. If serious, the liver and bloodstream become overloaded with fat, and the whole body goes into shock.
- Do not be tempted to have the shoes removed, especially if the soles are flat.
- Do not use anything that applies direct pressure to the sole.
- Do not force the horse to exercise in the belief that this will encourage circulation in the foot; it is more likely to cause further traumatic tearing of the laminae.

Proper sole support (as provided by deep, soft bedding) and complete box rest are probably the two most important factors to a successful outcome.

Chronic laminitis does not need to be treated with quite the same urgency, but you should still contact your vet for advice.

WHAT WILL YOUR VET DO?

Your vet will want to establish the severity of the laminitis, how much damage has been done, and what the possible causes are. To achieve this, he or she will do some, or all, of the following:
- Ask you to give a full, recent history of your horse's

health, diet and working pattern, emphasising any recent changes.

- Perform a full clinical examination, bearing in mind that it is important to establish the presence of any co-existing illnesses or injuries elsewhere in the body.
- Take blood samples, and sometimes also urine samples, for laboratory analysis, to establish whether there are any other co-existing conditions.
- Assess the presence and severity of all the classic signs of laminitis previously mentioned.
- Take X-rays of the feet (see opposite).

There are additional, more sophisticated diagnostic techniques, which can provide considerable helpful information. At the present time, these are not usually readily available for routine evaluation, instead being used mainly for hospitalised cases or for research purposes. They inlude:

- **Digital venograms:** A means of visualising the blood circulation in the hoof capsule, by introducing a dye into the veins that can then be traced using X-rays. There are suggestions that this may have a therapeutic value, presumably flushing out the circulation.
- **Gamma or nuclear scintigraphy:** The use of a radioactive compound in the body to highlight areas of tissue damage.
- **Thermography:** The measurement of relative changes in body temperature associated with disease.
- **Computerised tomography (CT scan):** The use of a complex system of X-rays and radiation detectors to produce a detailed, computerised 3D image of both bone and soft tissue structures.
- **Magnetic resonance imaging (MRI):** The production of superior 3D images of inaccessible soft tissue structures, by measuring the energy

released from hydrogen nuclei in the body, previously
'excited' by the application of magnetic fields.

These techniques all provide information about the
state of the circulation within the foot, and, as such,
can be extremely valuable in assessing the severity of a
case. This enables a more accurate prognosis to be
given. They are also useful in monitoring cases, and so
assist in the validation of various treatments – hence
their importance in research.

X-RAYS

X-rays of the lateral foot are extremely important and
useful, as they provide invaluable information about
the relative anatomy of the bones within the foot.
They are, therefore, essential in assessing:

- The presence and degree of pedal bone rotation
- Possible prognosis (or outcome)
- Response to initial treatment
- Response to longer term, corrective foot care.

The majority of portable X-ray machines are quite
capable of producing a good image. This means that
most X-rays can be taken on the owner's premises
(providing power is available), eliminating the need to
move the horse unnecessarily. Many vets will elect to
carry out this procedure for the first time at some
stage during the initial three to four days of the disease,
and then repeat it at stages during rehabilitation for
monitoring purposes.

The foot needs to be clean and dry, with the frog
trimmed of any excess. A drawing pin is placed in the
frog approximately 0.4 inches (1 cm) back from its
point, and a stiff wire is taped along the front of the
hoof wall, ending at the top where the hard horn
becomes soft coronary band. These act as markers and

assist in the interpretation of the X-rays. They also help the farrier to assess how much should be trimmed and what size shoe to fit.

The developed X-rays will give information about:

- The presence and extent of any pedal bone rotation.
- The presence and extent of any distal displacement, or sinking, of the pedal bone – this can be very subtle and therefore difficult to assess.
- The presence of remodelling or 'lysis' of the pedal bone, signifying more chronic arthritic types of change.
- The presence of laminar thickening.
- The presence of gas accumulation beneath the front hoof wall, indicating previous episodes of laminar bleeding.

Once your veterinarian has diagnosed laminitis, he or she will suggest a range of treatments, depending on the severity and cause (see Chapter Four).

MARKERS USED WHEN TAKING FOOT X-RAYS

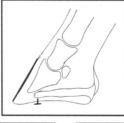

Wire taped to front of hoof wall

Drawing pin in apex of frog

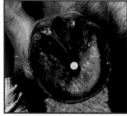

X-RAY RESULTS

'Normal' foot: P1, P2 and P3 are in a relatively straight line. The front of the hoof wall is parallel to the front of the pedal bone, which is at a relatively normal angle to the ground.

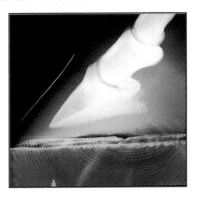

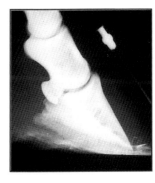

Early case of acute founder: The pedal bone has begun to rotate downwards as shown by the increased vertical distance betwen the top of the wire and the top of P3, and by the loss of the parallel relationship between the wire and the front of P3.

Severe chronic founder: The outline of the hoof can be seen to differ hugely from the positioning of the pedal bone, which has moved so far back in the foot that it is resting behind the apex of the frog.

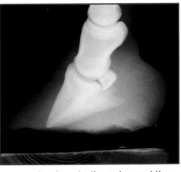

The point of P3 is dangerously close to the sole, and the horse is literally walking on the tips of its pedal bones.

4 Treatment

Generally, treatment can be divided into immediate, short-term 'emergency' treatment (which tends to be medical) and longer-term treatment (which tends to involve more in the way of therapeutic foot care).

In many cases, treatment can be prolonged and extremely costly, with no guarantee of success. Your vet will want to discuss all the implications with you at an early stage. Insurance may play a vital role in reaching decisions at this time.

Below are some of the points that are important to grasp when trying to appreciate the complexities of the disease and the implications of treatment:

- By the time the clinical signs appear, much of the damage has already been done.
- The final outcome is impossible to predict.
- Treatment may be necessary for the horse's lifetime.
- Even if the initial response is good, further episodes of laminitis or other foot problems are possible.
- Horses may appear sound, even though the damage is still there.
- If complications occur, the horse may require special care on an almost daily basis for the rest of its life.

The exact form of treatment your vet provides will depend on a number a factors. *There is no single correct treatment that covers all aspects*, and every case of laminitis is different. This is why there are so many treatment options available, and little way of knowing, in advance, which will be most suitable.

INITIAL MANAGEMENT

The horse or pony should have been moved on to deep bedding in a comfortable stable already. It is unfortunate that some owners still believe that it is sufficient just to rope off a section of the paddock.

If it is known that the laminitis is due to over-consumption of concentrates (e.g. breaking into the feed bins), the vet may elect to stomach tube the patient and administer a dose of liquid paraffin (with or without epsom salts). This will certainly help to flush out any remaining grain in the intestines but, unfortunately, it is usually a case of 'shutting the stable door after the horse has bolted'. The damage will have been done already by the time laminitis signs appear.

TREATING THE PRIMARY PROBLEM

As we know, many cases of laminitis are secondary to a primary problem elsewhere in the body. This may be a serious, life-threatening illness and it is essential that it should be treated too. This may involve the use of:

- Intensive antibiotic therapy
- Intravenous fluids with or without electrolytes
- Manual procedures (e.g. removal of retained placenta).

Clearly, if the horse or pony is seriously ill, it would be better for him or her to be hospitalised, so that intensive therapy can be carried out more efficiently.

MEDICAL TREATMENT

Medical therapy is aimed at reducing the pain and inflammation in the foot, and improving the blood circulation. Together, this will help to stabilise the situation and to prevent further functional destruction.

There are a large number of treatment options available and every vet will have his or her preferred regime.

Anti-inflammatories/painkillers

These invaluable drugs lessen pain and reduce inflammation and blood pressure within the foot. They are often used long term and are an essential part of therapy. Very occasionally they can cause ulcers and bleeding in the intestines. They can also make an animal appear better than it really is. Ideally, they should, therefore, be used only at a dose low enough to lessen the pain, but not to abolish it altogether – and no recovering animal should be allowed exercise unless it has been off all forms of painkiller for at least 7 days. The drugs available include:

- Phenylbutazone or 'bute' (the most popular anti-inflammatory in use, e.g. Equipalazone, Prodynam).
- Meclofenamate (e.g. Arquel, Equafen).
- Flunixin meglumine (e.g. Finadyne).
- Salicylate acid (e.g. aspirin).
- Dimethyl sulphoxide (DMSO).

Vasodilators

These drugs help the blood vessels to relax and dilate, so improving the ease of blood flow and lowering the blood pressure within the foot. They include acepromazine (e.g. ACP) and isoxsuprine (e.g. Circulon, Duviculine). ACP has the added benefit of being a sedative, which encourages the patient to lie down.

Anti-clotting agents (anti-coagulants)

These drugs help to prevent the formation of blood clots, the presence of which can cause further blockage and disruption to the delicate circulation within the foot. They include heparin sulphate and aspirin.

Miscellaneous drug treatments

There are a large number of other drugs available that

claim to have a role to play. Some have no scientific proof as to their efficacy as yet, and some are currently available only in the USA. They include:

- Glycerine trinitrite: Used as ointments or pads on the pasterns, these claim to have a direct vasodilatory effect due to their nitric oxide content.
- Vedaprofen: An anti-endotoxic drug that counteracts the destructive effects of endotoxins on the foot.
- Phenoxybenzamine: This claims to be a good vasodilator and to prevent thrombosis.
- Pentoxiphylline: Given early, this drug alters the deformability of the red blood cells, enhancing their transport through the capillary beds in the foot.

FOOT CARE

It is vital to stabilise the foot to prevent any further mechanical failure from occurring. There are many thoughts on how to achieve this – with some proposals appearing to be directly contradictory to others. Your vet will follow the course of action that he or she believes to be most appropriate for your particular case.

Short-term, therapeutic foot care is aimed at reducing the damaging shearing forces on the hoof walls and the interlocking laminar system. It also aims to decrease the pressure of an unstable pedal bone on the sole beneath. This can be achieved by recruiting other parts of the foot's ground surface (e.g. the frog) to bear weight, so that the stresses on the wall are lessened and the laminae are prevented from tearing further. This prevents additional displacement of the pedal bone.

There are several ways of increasing the ground contact between the frog, sole, and the bars in the back two-thirds of the foot:

- Stabling on deep, soft bedding, such as shavings, soft sand or even mud. This will provide uniform pressure to the frog and sole.

- Removing the shoes (providing the sole has not become flat or convex). Shoes can be detrimental in a case of laminitis, as they raise the sole, exaggerating the pedal bone's potential for sinking. Shoes transfer all the weight-bearing role on to the hoof walls. However, if the sole has dropped, the shoes should be left on, as they are providing some protection in this situation. Owners should not be tempted to wrench off shoes themselves, as this will cause further tearing to the laminae. Consult your vet or farrier.

- Using 'frog support pads'. These are pads of soft material that are placed over the frog and then bound in place. They may be made out of rolls of bandage, rubber, tights or anything else to hand. Alternatively, commercially produced frog pads, called 'lily pads', are available.

- Packing the sole. This can be done with materials such as gypsum, rubber impression material, or styrofoam. This approach is very popular, but there remain concerns that packing out the sole is potentially hazardous and that good, soft bedding will be just as effective.

- Putting the foot in a cast: This remains controversial, as there is potential for complications.

- Corrective foot trimming where needed (see page 37).

- Bevelling or rounding off the toe. This increases the

Although frog support pads can be useful in the management of laminitis, it is important that they are placed on the foot correctly, to prevent 'bed sore' type lesions developing.

ease of foot break over (the final part of the weight-bearing phase of the foot, just before the toe leaves the ground), and, therefore, reduces further the stresses on the front wall of the foot.

- Elevating the heel. This loosens the tension in the deep digital flexor tendon, which contributes in pulling the pedal bone out of position. As with placing the foot in a cast, this remains controversial, and is only really of use in acute cases that have not already foundered. If pedal bone rotation has occurred, raising the heel could add to the compression and damage of the coronary corium.

- Dorsal wall drilling. In some cases, fluid gathers underneath the front hoof wall as a result of haemorrhage and leakage from the damaged blood vessels in the laminae there. Pressure builds up until it becomes very painful (similar to a blood blister under one's nail). In such circumstances, dorsal wall drilling can be performed, whereby a small drill is bored into the front of the foot, releasing the fluid and thereby relieving the pressure and pain. This procedure is usually delayed until at least one week into the illness, so that it does not have to be repeated.

LONGER-TERM TREATMENT

It is vital to appreciate that there is no single treatment or shoe that works for all cases when managing chronic cases of laminitis, as every case can have many variables. Once again, it is essential to discuss expectations, goals and the economics of the situation from the start. In some cases, it is immediately clear that the severity of the attack, combined with other considerations (such as cost), means that treatment is unlikely to be successful. In such cases, a decision for euthanasia is better made sooner rather than later.

It is also essential that you have a committed vet and farrier who are prepared to work together. Treating the chronically laminitic animal is very much a team effort.

NURSING
Be aware that your animal may be in considerable and constant pain, despite all attempts at control. Tender loving care ('TLC') and considerate nursing will go a long way towards recovery.

MEDICAL TREATMENT
Painkillers (e.g. bute), and, to a lesser extent, vasodilators (e.g. ACP), may be continued for several weeks.

EXERCISE
Many cases will need to remain on complete box rest for a considerable number of weeks, and certainly until they are moving happily without painkillers. Exercise should then be gradually introduced, keeping to soft ground wherever possible – an all-weather school is ideal. Avoid surfaces that could traumatise the foot, such as uneven rock and frozen ground.

Exercise remains a subject of considerable debate, with some believing that it genuinely helps with the recovery process, and others insisting that it is too risky if allowed too soon. It would be fair to say that your horse is less likely to have a relapse if stabled, as opposed to turned out, and that prolonged box rest is, therefore, the safest option – but every case is different and you should be guided by your vet.

FOOT CARE
This is probably the most important aspect of longer-term treatment. Therapeutic foot care is now aimed at trying to restore the normal alignment and shape of

the foot, or, in cases where the problems are irreversible, helping the animal to exist with permanent structural damage. A good farrier becomes an invaluable asset. The necessary foot care cannot be carried out in just one visit – it is more likely that attention will be needed regularly every four to five weeks for many months, and this all adds to the cost. Further X-rays, taken at regular intervals, will help to monitor progress.

Once again, there is a huge range of options available and what is done will depend on the individual case.

Corrective foot trimming

The foot needs to be trimmed to try to re-establish the parallel relationship between the front of the pedal bone and the front of the hoof wall. This usually involves:

- Taking the toes well back (called 'dressing the foot forward'). This may require that the hoof wall is rasped right back to the distorted laminae beneath.
- Removing excessive heel growth. Your farrier will judge how much toe and heel to take off by assessing the angle of the most recent horn from the side, and from studying the X-rays that should be available.

Therapeutic shoeing

It is generally agreed that the foot is better off with some sort of support rather than leaving it unshod.

Many types of therapeutic shoeing regimes are available, with some being more controversial than others. In all cases, the aim is to support the walls, provide cover at the heels, and to encourage other parts of the foot's ground surface to take some of the weight, without putting pressure directly on the sole itself. It is essential to have the foot X-rayed if you want your farrier to be able to fit a therapeutic shoe accurately. Many types of shoe are also available as plastic, glue-on commercial kits, so avoiding the painful and possibly damaging effects of having to nail clenches into the foot.

Regularly used therapeutic shoes include:

- Egg-bar shoes: Completely oval or egg-shaped shoes that provide plenty of cover and support at the heels.

- Heart-bar shoes: Bar shoes with an extension from the heels to cover and make contact with the frog, so including the frog as part of the ground surface of the foot. There are many varieties, including adjustable heart-bar shoes that have a hinge to the heart-bar part, allowing alterations to the frog pressure to be made; and systems using heart-bars in combination with pads and rubber-like impression material (e.g. the Equine Digit Support System). However, heart-bar shoes should be fitted only under certain circumstances and only when X-rays are available, so consult your vet and farrier first.

- Back-to-front or open-toed shoes: These can be of help, especially if the front of the foot has had to be rasped back severely. There are concerns that the long-term use of these shoes could contribute to contraction of the deep digital flexor tendon.

- Sole pads: The use of these is controversial. They

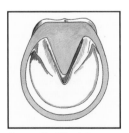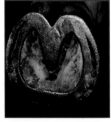

Correctly fitted (represented above left and in practice above right) heart-bar shoes can be a big help in certain cirumstances.

claim to increase the stability of the pedal bone, improve the rigidity of the sole and hoof wall as a unit, and aid in protecting the solar surface. However, many claim that any sort of direct solar pressure could be damaging. Using an impression material under the pad helps to reduce this risk.

- Wedges: Heel wedges can help to counteract the pull of the deep digital flexor tendon, although there are thoughts that this could ultimately contribute to a permanent contraction of the tendon. Elevating the toe with toe wedges can assist in restoring the normal alignment of the pedal bone.
- Modified toes: Rocker, square, rolled and 4-point toes can all help by lessening the pull of the deep digital flexor tendon, and by reducing the breakover stresses on the front of the hoof wall.

It is worth remembering that, with many chronic cases, the feet are unlikely to become fully structurally normal even if they become fully functionally normal.

Dorsal wall resection

In some cases, it may be necessary to remove the whole of the front of the hoof:

- If a large amount of fluid has formed under the wall from capillary damage, haemorrhage and leakage.
- If the fluid is reabsorbed, leaving area of gas.
- If the hoof-wall capsule has become too weakened and detached by the acute episode.

This technique can be fairly aggressive, often requiring both a farrier and vet in attendance. It aids the situation by allowing:

- The release of painful pressure
- The removal of dead laminar tissue

- The drainage of infection
- New horn to grow down in the right position, parallel to the pedal bone
- The rebuilding of the hoof wall with artificial materials where necessary, until new horn has grown down, although this technique is no longer as popular as it once was, and many farriers feel it is unnecessary.

SURGERY

In some chronic cases, the deep digital flexor tendon becomes permanently contracted and shortened, preventing the pedal bone from being restored to its correct position. These animals tend to have very raised heels, giving the appearance that they are standing and walking on their toes. There are two surgical techniques available to correct this situation:

- Deep digital flexor tendon tenotomy. This involves cutting through the tendon at mid-cannon level. It can be performed under local or general aneasthesia.
- Inferior check ligament tenotomy. This can only be performed under a general anaesthetic. It appears to give the deep digital flexor tendon more laxity.

Both techniques tend to be utilised only as a last resort and as a salvage procedure for potential brood mares. Consistent surgical shoeing and a full year off are needed, but it is possible for some horses to return to ridden work afterwards.

DIETARY MANAGEMENT

Gone are the days when it was thought one should starve laminitic horses. While many cases need to lose weight, this must be done gradually, and it is important to keep the horse healthy and reasonably sated throughout the period of recovery.

During convalescence, your horse or pony should be fed on a complete forage diet, which provides roughage at 2 per cent of the body weight (or 1.5 per cent if the animal is overweight). There are many ways of achieving this, and your vet will be able to advise you.

Below is a suggestion of what could be included:

- Alfalfa (e.g. Alfa A). This is low in starch and sugar, and provides a good, balanced source of calcium, lysine and methionine, all of which are important for healthy hoof growth.
- An equal portion of chopped oat straw.
- Sloppy, unmolassed sugar-beet pulp, to bind together the alfalfa and chopped oat straw.
- Old hay (little and often).
- A hoof supplement, such as Farrier's Formula, which contains the ingredients for healthy hoof-wall growth, the three nutrients necessary for optimal liver function, and the precursors of thyroxine, which has a role in cases of hypothyroidism.
- Omega-3 fatty acids (e.g. soya or linseed oil) as a safer source of slow-release energy.
- A probiotic, such as live yeast culture. This improves fibre digestion by increasing the number of fibre digesting bacteria in the hind gut.

Many feed companies now produce high-fibre, low-starch commercial feeds especially for the laminitic animal. They carry the Laminitis Trust approval mark and make dietary management much more convenient. However, do not fall into the trap of believing that, just because they are approved, they are safe to feed in large quantities. This is not the case!

Some animals, especially ponies, become frustrated and bored with relatively meagre rations. Try to keep yours occupied by spreading the hay around the stable, so that the animal has to search for it. Also hang a swede or bunch of gorse from the ceiling for the horse to nibble at, and provide one of the many toys now available for incarcerated equines.

COMPLICATIONS

Infections or foot abscesses are a common complication of chronic laminitis. They tend to occur in the sole, as a result of solar bruising, or in the white line, where there has been laminar separation. In all cases, it is necessary to open up the abscess and allow it to drain. Treatment is usually fairly straightforward and satisfying, although more serious complications can occur.

If sinkers are to be saved, they need immediate attention. The pedal bone needs to be supported and restored in to position within a matter of hours, before the haemorrhage and oedema have caused irreversible mechanical failure.

RECOVERY

One of the first questions I am often asked when treating a case of laminitis is "Will I ever ride my horse again?". There is an understandable need for the vet to give an anxious owner some sort of prognosis. However, with so many variables and possibilities, and with no single treatment being better than another, it is very difficult to predict accurately what will happen.

While it is unrealistic of you to expect your vet to be able or willing to give a guaranteed and accurate prediction of the outcome, there are some factors that are recognised as being good or bad signs, and which go some way towards forming an informed prognosis. Your vet will discuss these with you.

The general outlook can be summarised as:
• Acute laminitis (without rotation): 100 per cent

chance of recovery
- Acute founder: 80 per cent chance of recovery
- Chronic founder: 60-80 per cent chance of recovery
- Sinker: 20 per cent chance of recovery.

The most difficult cases (therefore carrying the worst prognosis) have more than one of the following:
- Sinking of P3
- A solar prolapse with secondary infection of the pedal bone
- Chronic contraction of the joints of the lower limb, due to shortening of the deep digital flexor tendon.

EUTHANASIA

Sadly, some cases of chronic laminitis fail to respond, despite all attempts at rehabilitation. There are many possible reasons for this, which include:
- A permanently distorted foot circulation
- Chronic irreversible rotation
- Excessive bruising
- Chronic infection of P3
- Arthritis of P3
- Wastage of P3 due to prolonged disuse or pressure.

These animals will be in permanent discomfort and, ultimately, it is kinder to have them euthanased than watch them struggle on. Sadly, many chronic cases are allowed to continue with their painful lives simply because their owners cannot bear to make the decision to have them put down. The humane and ethical issues are complex, but ultimately one must consider the long-term welfare of the animal. The fact that he or she is still eating does not mean that they are free of pain. Be guided by your vet, and remind yourself that you are doing the best for your horse or pony.

5 Prevention

U p to 80 per cent of laminitis cases are consequences of faults in management, and therefore, can be prevented.

DIETARY MANAGEMENT

Over-feeding is extremely common, especially among native ponies that have evolved to live on moorland or mountains with poor grazing throughout the year.

Below are some of the things to consider when planning your animal's feeding regime:

- Feed according to work: Most native ponies and many horses can live and perform basic work, including hacking, on a forage-only diet.
- Increase work load *before* increasing the food level.
- Give a 'hard' feed (e.g. nuts, coarse mix) only if work demands it. 'Cooked' or 'extruded' feeds contain more digestible starch, and are, therefore, safer.
- If you use feed as a 'reward', use a handful of chaff or alfalfa, plus a carrot, instead of nuts or mix.
- It is best to avoid anything high in water-soluble carbohydrates (e.g. lush grass, new hay and cereals, especially if these are highly molassed).
- Feed high-fibre feeds (not high-calorie) that are low in starch and sugar (available as chops, nuts, mixes or chaffs). Look for the Laminitis Trust approval mark.

CONTROLLING WEIGHT

- Remember that 'fat is *not* fit' – feed little and often.
- Include a supplement that promotes healthy hoof-wall growth.

- Consider using a probiotic prior to a known time of stress, such as a long journey.
- Control grazing opportunities, especially during the high-risk times of spring and summer.
- Have a small 'weight watchers' paddock available, or a sand school for turnout.
- Strip graze using electric fencing.
- Pre-graze with cattle or sheep.
- Use a grazing muzzle, which has a slot in the bottom to allow drinking. Remember to check the field for any hazards, such as old baths with taps, which the muzzle could get caught on.
- Turn out susceptible ponies for short periods of only one to two hours during the day if you are unable to restrict their access.
- Do not be misled into thinking that, if you keep your horse stabled during the day, it will be safe to turn it on to ad-lib grass at night. It won't be! Horses and ponies often graze for longer, uninterrupted periods at night, especially if it is cool and they are hungry.
- If your horse is very hungry, give some hay or chaff, dampened with molasses, before turning out. This will help to stop it from over-eating, and the presence of fibre in the bowels will help to slow the movement of soluble carbohydrates.
- Manage your fields so that they have a high leaf-to-stem ratio. Traditional meadow-type pasture is lower in fructans and methionine than reseeded grassland.
- Avoid turning out on cold, sunny mornings until the frost has gone and fructan levels have lessened.
- Avoid turning out on to stubble after a hay crop, because of the high levels of fructans in the stems.
- Remember that grass is not dangerous in itself. It is

only dangerous if the fructan concentration is high and if too much is consumed. It is incorrect to believe that a chronically laminitic animal can never be allowed to graze again.

- Learn to recognise if your animal is getting over weight. Grey ponies seem to be especially susceptible. Fat animals have thick, hard, cresty necks, fat in front of the udder in mares, or a thick pendulous sheath in geldings and stallions, and ribs that cannot be felt easily.

- Invest in a girth weigh-tape, from which you can assess your horse's condition and monitor it regularly.

- Always ensure that you can feel your animal's ribs and that its condition does not rise above a score of 3 (on a scale of 1 to 5, with 1 being emaciated and 5 being obese).

- Try to get your horse lean before turning out in spring (i.e. you should be able to feel the ribs, but not necessarily see them). A horse premanently on spring grass cannot easily be dieted, and if your animal comes through the winter fat, it is going to be very difficult to control its weight for the rest of the year.

- Remember to worm and pick up droppings regularly.

- Consider using a product called Founderguard, available from your vet only after a special licence has been applied for. Founderguard contains the antibiotic virginiamycin, which prevents the excess growth of lactate-producing bacteria in the hind gut following the ingestion of excessive amounts of soluble carbohydrate. It is designed to be fed on a daily basis as a preventative measure, in addition to the usual dietary control regimes, and it should not be considered a treatment.

FOOT CARE

The saying "no foot, no horse" is very true, and it is clear that the risks of laminitis are greater if the feet are in a bad or neglected condition. Consider the following:

- Keep the toes on the front feet well trimmed. This helps to lessen the mechanical tearing of weakened laminae by the lever action of the foot, especially in those animals with naturally long toes and low heels.
- Keep the feet regularly shod.
- Stable on clean, dry bedding at all times.
- Use a supplement such as Farrier's Formula to promote good, strong horn growth.
- Avoid excessive concussion (e.g. trotting on the roads).
- Ride regularly.
- Consider the benefits of having your horse's feet X-rayed routinely once a year. This is an excellent way of picking up potential problems in the very early stages, before serious and perhaps irreversible damage has occurred.

INSURANCE

Treating a laminitic animal can become expensive, and insurance is invaluable in these situations. Insurance is the owner's responsibilty, although your vet will be happy to discuss it with you. Bear in mind that, following an attack of laminitis, most insurance companies will understandably put an exclusion clause on any claims for further episodes of laminitis.

6 Myths and legends

Below are some of the old wives' tales about laminitis that are frequently heard:
- "Forced walking will help": This can cause further laminar damage and great distess to the horse.
- "Only the front legs are ever involved": Any combination of legs can be involved, although laminitis is most common in the front legs.
- "Drinking cold water after exercise can cause laminitis": There is no evidence of a direct connection, although it can cause colic.
- "Laminitis is an allergy": No evidence supports this.
- "A pregnant mare cannot get laminitis": A pregnant mare is just as much at risk.
- "Heat in the foot always indicates laminitis": Heat is a very inconsistent finding.
- "Laminitics should be stood in streams or coldwater hosed": This is not of any benefit unless it is done very early on, during the developmental stage, when it is desirable to reduce the blood flow to the foot. Following this, it is actually more desirable to use hot water on the foot, to encourage the circulation to 'open up'.
- "Cutting the jugular vein and bleeding the animal helps": This can lower blood pressure in the feet, but it is drastic and can have unfortunate complications.
- "You should starve a laminitic": This is not only unfair, it is also potentially dangerous.
- "Laminitis is hereditary": There is no proof of this.

Never rely on old wives' tales. Always consult your vet.